Samuel French Acting Edition

The Strang

by Agatha Christie

SAMUELFRENCH.COM   SAMUELFRENCH.CO.UK

ISBN 978-0-573-03108-3

concordtheatricals.co.uk
concordtheatricals.com
www.agathachristielimited.com

FOR PRODUCTION ENQUIRIES

UNITED KINGDOM AND WORLD
EXCLUDING NORTH AMERICA
licensing@concordtheatricals.co.uk
020-7054-7200

UNITED STATES AND CANADA
Info@concordtheatricals.com
1-866-979-0447

Each title is subject to availability from Samuel French,
depending upon country of performance.

MUSIC USE NOTE

Licensees are solely responsible for obtaining formal written permission from copyright owners to use copyrighted music in the performance of this play and are strongly cautioned to do so. If no such permission is obtained by the licensee, then the licensee must use only original music that the licensee owns and controls. Licensees are solely responsible and liable for all music clearances and shall indemnify the copyright owners of the play(s) and their licensing agent, Samuel French, against any costs, expenses, losses and liabilities arising from the use of music by licensees. Please contact the appropriate music licensing authority in your territory for the rights to any incidental music.

IMPORTANT BILLING AND CREDIT REQUIREMENTS

If you have obtained performance rights to this title, please refer to your licensing agreement for important billing and credit requirements.

CHARACTERS

DORIS WEST
MRS. HUGGINS
ENID BRADSHAW
GERALD STRANGE
DICK LANE
MRS. BIRCH

NOTES ON CASTING

Doris West or Mrs. Huggins may double with Mrs. Birch.

Minimum number of performers: 5.

SETTING

ACT I

A flat in Kensington.

ACT II

The living room of a cottage in the country.

ACT III

Same as Act II.

TIME

ACT I

A morning in spring.

ACT II

An afternoon three months later.

ACT III

The same evening.

ACT I

(A flat in Kensington. A morning in spring. A pleasant, rather cheaply furnished sitting room with chairs, a writing desk, and a bookcase. There is a door that leads to the hall, another that leads to the bedrooms and another that leads to the dining room and kitchen. **DORIS WEST**, *a nondescript girl of twenty-eight, is sitting at the desk. She tears up a sheet of paper and throws it in a waste paper basket.* **MRS. HUGGINS**, *a middle-aged woman, is polishing.)*

DORIS. Get me another waste paper basket, will you, Mrs. Huggins? This one is full up.

MRS. HUGGINS. Yes, Miss.

(She takes the waste paper basket.)

And shall I bring you a cup of tea, Miss? The kettle is on and it is just eleven o'clock.

DORIS. Eleven o'clock? Already!

MRS. HUGGINS. Eleven it is, Miss.

(She exits into the kitchen. **DORIS** *looks around the room.)*

DORIS. The way one keeps things is really idiotic.

(She sighs as though admonishing herself.)

There, get on with what you are doing. Don't be an idiot.

*(***MRS. HUGGINS** *enters with a tray of tea.)*

MRS. HUGGINS. Here you are, Miss.

(She looks around the room.)

MRS. HUGGINS. Well, everything is about finished now.

DORIS. *(Sighing.)* Yes.

MRS. HUGGINS. Ah, you're right, Miss. It doesn't look near as nice as it did with all your pretty things about. But there, it is good enough for tenants. Some of the things you hear. Why, you would hardly believe –

DORIS. *(Distantly.)* Really?

MRS. HUGGINS. Such deceit and wickedness! Going away without paying up! Well, that you are on the look out for, but a lady as I did for, very particular she was too, as to who she let to – no children or dogs – well, would you believe it, she let to as nice spoken a lady as you could imagine and went away to the Riviera and when she came back, the flat was empty – empty, Miss! Carted off all the furniture in a van she had and sold it.

DORIS. Well, I hope we shan't strike a tenant like that.

MRS. HUGGINS. You never know, Miss.

(She pauses.)

What I mean to say is, you can't tell – not by looks and not by references.

DORIS. Well, let's try and look at the bright side, Mrs. Huggins.

MRS. HUGGINS. As I always do, Miss. Well known I am for it. Ah, they say – Mrs. Huggins is always one to make the best of things. What I say is, there's always a silver lining to every cloud. And so I've told Huggins many a time when he's had a disappointment over what won the 3:30. And I will say, Miss, that it's my belief that horses are very artful. You never know what they're going to do till they've done it – so to speak. And men is much the same. To see the way these young girls go about believing every word a man says to them, it makes my heart bleed for them – fairly bleed.

*(**DORIS** is absorbed in a letter.)*

DORIS. Um – yes – yes, of course.

MRS. HUGGINS. Ah, well, they soon find out what's what and get resigned to it, so to speak. I hope now, as Miss Enid's young gentleman won't be too much of a disappointment to her. From his photograph on her dressing table he looks a nice, quiet gentleman – the steady sort. But then, for all his quiet look, he may be a secret drinker or something like that.

DORIS. *(Smiling.)* Mr. Lane doesn't drink, Mrs. Huggins.

MRS. HUGGINS. That's just the kind of thing you can't be sure about, Miss – begging your pardon. Gentlemen who come back from foreign parts like Mr. Lane, well, they do acquire the habit, there's no denying it. And foreign wives as often as not! Ah! There's a lot of wickedness goes on in the tropics. I've known as quiet and steady a young gentleman as you could imagine – a total abstainer when he went out – come back and not be able to leave the whisky alone. If I were you, Miss, I'd prepare Miss Enid. She's a nice young lady and I wouldn't like her to get too much of a shock.

DORIS. All right. I'll tell her that a bloated dipsomaniac may roll in.

MRS. HUGGINS. It's a long time since she's seen him.

DORIS. Three years since he was last home.

MRS. HUGGINS. Dear, dear, and them engaged seven years. It reminds one of the Bible, it does. A real romance, I call it. Them two, waiting faithfully for each other all those years. Ah, Miss, I do hope and pray, as she mayn't be disappointed in him.

DORIS. Well, at any rate, she knows something about him after all these years. Seven years is a good long time.

MRS. HUGGINS. Seven years or seventy – you never know with a man. Men is always men.

DORIS. Oh, come Mrs. Huggins. I hope it won't be as bad as all that. After all, if you don't know what a man is like after seven or eight years, when will you know?

MRS. HUGGINS. Never! Secretive, that's what men are – and artful. You never know what they are thinking and planning until they are in their graves.

DORIS. (*Slyly.*) Dear me, is Huggins...?

MRS. HUGGINS. Oh, Huggins! I made it clear to Huggins that I'd stand no nonsense!

DORIS. I see.

MRS. HUGGINS. Miss Enid will be wise to do the same. Put your foot down at the start. It's the only way. But there, Miss Enid is a gentle creature.

> (*She collects the tea things and exits into the kitchen.* DORIS *speaks softly to herself.*)

DORIS. She's one in a hundred. One in a hundred.

> (MRS. HUGGINS *re-enters with a duster.*)

MRS. HUGGINS. Ah, it's a sad time for you, Miss, as we all know.

DORIS. Yes. I shall miss Enid terribly.

MRS. HUGGINS. Four years you've shared this flat and I really and truly do believe that you've never once had, what I should call, a proper dust up.

DORIS. No, we've never quarrelled. That's pretty good, isn't it, Mrs. Huggins?

MRS. HUGGINS. It's all right for two ladies, Miss. Husband and wife is different. A good row clears the air, that's what I always say. Go for each other at the start and maybe you'll have a peaceful old age. Why, the first year me and Huggins were married he didn't rightly know whether he was on his head or his heels.

DORIS. Does he know now?

MRS. HUGGINS. He's learnt as I won't be trifled with.

DORIS. Mrs. Huggins, I believe you bully poor Huggins unmercifully.

MRS. HUGGINS. Well, it's got to be one way or the other. I've seen to it as he doesn't bully me. And he's nothing to complain of – clean as a new pin I keep things – and his meals hot and tasty. But be firm with a man you must be. And so I'd advise Miss Enid, if she wouldn't think it impertinence.

DORIS. According to you, Mrs. Huggins, married life is a perpetual battle.

MRS. HUGGINS. And so it is, Miss. With one party always defeated. And what I say is this: take care as you're the winning party from the start! As I say, Miss Enid's a gentle creature and it's my fear as she may start wrong.

DORIS. She is a gentle creature.

MRS. HUGGINS. And yet though, for all that, she's secretive. You never know what she's really thinking or feeling. Why, look at her this morning! Here's her young gentleman coming home after all these years – and them going to get married at once – and her, as calm and ordinary as you please. Not even excited looking.

DORIS. What do you expect her to do? Dance about and sing?

MRS. HUGGINS. I know she's one to hide her feelings – and of course, there are them as takes their pleasures sadly. And sad is what she looked this morning in my opinion.

DORIS. *(Thoughtfully.)* So, you thought she looked sad, too.

MRS. HUGGINS. Well, she's probably right. As I say, you never know with marriage.

DORIS. She did look sad – and I want her so much to be happy. Oh, she must be happy!

MRS. HUGGINS. There's no real happiness this side of the grave, they say.

DORIS. I wish I were sure –

> *(She breaks off anxiously. Taking a pile of letters, she exits to the bedrooms.* **MRS. HUGGINS** *sings* in a tuneless voice whilst dusting.)*

MRS. HUGGINS.

THOUGH I SAY NOT WHAT I MAY NOT LET YOU HEAR,

---

* A license to produce *The Stranger* does not include a performance license for any third-party or copyrighted music. Licensees should create an original composition or use music in the public domain. For further information, please see Music Use Note on page 3.

STILL THE TUM TI TUM TI TUM TI TUM TI LOVE ME, DEAR.

(The front door is heard.)

FOR I AM A DUTIFUL WIFE,
TUM TI TUM TI TUM TI TUM TI TUM TI,
IT BRINGS YOU BUT TROUBLE AND DANGER,
TO LISTEN TO LOVE FROM A STRANGER.

*(**ENID BRADSHAW** enters from the hall. She carries flowers. She is a rather pretty girl of twenty-eight.)*

ENID. Don't you do it, Mrs. Huggins.

MRS. HUGGINS. What, Miss?

ENID. Listen to 'Love From A Stranger.'

MRS. HUGGINS. It's a song, Miss, from *The Merry Widow*.

ENID. But you're not a merry widow. Think of Huggins.

MRS. HUGGINS. You will have your joke, Miss. Ah well, there's a lot of truth in that song. Listening to 'Love From A Stranger' has ruined many a poor young girl's life.

*(**ENID** unties the flowers.)*

ENID. Get me the tall glass and the round bowl, will you, Mrs. Huggins?

MRS. HUGGINS. Yes, Miss.

*(She exits to the kitchen. **DORIS** enters from the bedrooms.)*

DORIS. Hullo! You back? Oh, those flowers are rather lovely!

ENID. Yes, aren't they? What time is it?

DORIS. About a quarter past eleven.

*(**MRS. HUGGINS** enters with the vases.)*

What time will Dick get here?

ENID. About half past twelve, I should think. Thank you, Mrs. Huggins.

DORIS. You are not going to meet his train?

ENID. *(Shortly.)* No.

(**MRS. HUGGINS** *returns to the kitchen.*)

DORIS. You must be feeling awfully excited.

(**ENID** *does not answer.* **DORIS** *watches her with interest as she arranges the flowers.*)

ENID. There, I think that looks all right.

DORIS. Awfully nice.

ENID. How have you got on?

DORIS. I've just finished.

(*She pulls out the drawers of the desk.*)

All clear. I've just been enlivened by the cheery conversation of Mrs. Huggins.

ENID. Always the little ray of sunshine, I suppose?

DORIS. Oh, yes! She suggested that Dick had a foreign wife! That he drank! And that – anyway, you never knew.

(**ENID** *smiles.*)

Oh and by the way, she strongly advises you to put your foot down from the start – marriage being a battle.

ENID. (*Bitterly.*) I don't think my marriage is likely to be a battle.

DORIS. No. Dick's the sort of person one would feel awfully safe with.

ENID. Devastatingly so.

DORIS. Well, that's awfully satisfactory. I mean, I'm awfully fond of you, old girl. I wouldn't like you to take any risks.

ENID. I'm not taking any risk.

(*She looks round the room.*)

It doesn't look as attractive with the things put away, but it's still a very nice flat and ought to let easily.

DORIS. Did you go to the agents?

ENID. Yes. They seemed to think it would let quite easily.

DORIS. We're not asking very much for it but I think that's wise. If you ask too much, it frightens people away and they won't even come and look at it.

ENID. You're sure that you want to let it?

DORIS. Yes. I couldn't go on living here alone just at once. In six months or so it will be different.

ENID. I'm sorry, Doris.

DORIS. That's all right. Of course, I want you to be happy. I'm not a dog in the manger. I'm so awfully glad to think of you being happy after all these years of toiling and moiling in that old office.

ENID. I know. It's marvellous to feel free.

DORIS. Very thoughtful of your old cousin Jane to pop off when she did and leave you that five thousand.

ENID. And there are people who say money doesn't matter! Think of having £250 a year of my very own.

DORIS. I suppose without it, you and Dick couldn't have got married.

ENID. Oh yes, I think we could. But it will make a difference. We shan't have to pinch and scrape now.

DORIS. Enid, dear, I am so excited – about your getting married, I mean.

ENID. Why? There's nothing to get excited about.

(**DORIS** *stares at her.*)

DORIS. How queer you are.

ENID. No, I'm not.

DORIS. You are. I should have thought you'd have been all excited with Dick coming home after all these years. It's so romantic.

ENID. Is it romantic?

(*She pauses.*)

Or is it damnable?

DORIS. Enid!

(**ENID** *exits hurriedly to the bedrooms.* **DORIS** *stares after her as* **MRS. HUGGINS** *enters busily from the kitchen.*)

MRS. HUGGINS. I think I've finished now, Miss. Unless Miss Enid would like a nice cup of tea? The kettle's still on.

DORIS. No, I don't think she wants any tea.

MRS. HUGGINS. Shall I ask her, Miss?

DORIS. No, I shouldn't bother her. She seems rather upset.

MRS. HUGGINS. Oh... Still waters run deep, as they say. All right, Miss, I'll clear up in the kitchen and pop on my things and be off.

> *(She exits to the kitchen.* **DORIS** *looks anxiously towards the bedrooms.* **ENID** *enters.)*

ENID. Cheer up, Doris. Don't look so gloomy. I was only joking.

DORIS. Were you?

ENID. Of course. I'm really quite the excited young bride-to-be, with a correctly palpitating heart.

DORIS. Oh, Enid dear, don't. Not with me.

> *(A pause. They look at each other.)*

ENID. I don't know what's the matter. I can't understand myself.

DORIS. You're unhappy?

ENID. No, it's not that I'm unhappy exactly. But it's all so dull.

DORIS. Dull?

ENID. Yes, dull. Dick and I are fond of each other, and we've known each other for years, and we are well suited – but there isn't anything more! It's such a very tepid romance.

> *(***DORIS*** *looks at her in dismay.)*

When I came in, old Mother Huggins was bent double singing in that awful voice of hers about love from a stranger – and I realised that I wish Dick was a stranger.

DORIS. A stranger?

ENID. Yes. I wished that he wasn't dear old Dick, whom I knew so well. I wanted him to be strange and exciting and full of unknown possibilities.

DORIS. *(Shocked.)* Oh dear!

ENID. Don't worry. I'm sure lots of girls feel like this, but they marry and settle down and live happily ever afterwards.

DORIS. I feel you'll be so safe with Dick.

ENID. *(Drily.)* You're saying the wrong thing, Doris. At the moment I don't feel I want to be safe. Life's been so deadly monotonous. Day after day, year after year. Getting up in the morning, having to be in time at the office – the neat efficient secretary. Yes Mr. Cohen, no Mr. Cohen, certainly Mr. Cohen. Going out to lunch, rushing back. Girls in buses, reading novels – beastly, trashy stuff most of it. Yes – but exciting! Excitement, that's what we are all starved of. Day after day and nothing ever happens. Something exciting, thrilling, dangerous, absorbing. Oh, I want to live – to live before I am grey and old and dead!

DORIS. You've got Dick.

ENID. Yes, Dick.

DORIS. But look here, Enid. You – you do love Dick?

ENID. *(Frowning.)* Do I? Have I ever loved Dick or did I just think that he would do? It's an ugly thought, but it might be true. My only chance of romance, so I took it.

*(The telephone rings. **DORIS** answers it.)*

DORIS. Yes... Yes, speaking... Oh! Yes I think so – just a minute.

(She covers the phone.)

Someone wants to see the flat – a Mr. Strange. He would like to come along now, if it is convenient.

ENID. That'll be all right. If you'll go out and get the things we want for lunch, I'll stay here.

*(**DORIS** returns to the telephone.)*

DORIS. That will be quite convenient, thank you.

(She hangs up and looks at her watch.)

What's the time? Oh, good, it's not a quarter to twelve yet. Heaps of time –

(She makes to exit but hesitates.)

Enid –

ENID. It's all right. The storm is over. Nerves, darling. Just nerves. You go along.

(DORIS exits to the bedrooms. ENID looks in the mirror over the fireplace, speaking to her reflection.)

You are a damned fool.

(She goes to the bookcase and removes a volume. DORIS enters from the bedrooms ready to go out.)

DORIS. I don't suppose I shall be very long. Now mind, Enid, I shall expect you to have let the flat to this Mr. Strange by the time I come back.

ENID. I'll do my best. He shan't escape from me easily, I promise you.

(DORIS laughs and exits to the hall. The front door is heard. ENID opens the book. MRS. HUGGINS enters from the kitchen.)

MRS HUGGINS. I'm just going to pop round the corner for them cushions from the cleaners, Miss. Sure there's nothing else you want? You ought to have had a cup of tea, Miss Enid.

ENID. No thanks, Mrs. Huggins.

MRS. HUGGINS. Ah, you're not like me, Miss. If I miss my cup of tea at eleven, something seems wrong with the whole day. Though as far as that goes, there never is a day that goes quite right, is there, Miss?

ENID. Oh, I hope there is sometimes.

(She looks down at the book.)

I suppose you've never read the *Arabian Nights*, Mrs. Huggins?

MRS. HUGGINS. Now, I do remember something about it, Miss. "Sinbad the Sailor" and the "Old Man of the Sea," which I have often said to Huggins, as he is mine. Ah, there's no need to go to outlandish parts to have an Old Man of the Sea round your neck – as many a working woman can tell you.

ENID. Would you like to go to 'outlandish parts,' as you call them, Mrs. Huggins?

MRS. HUGGINS. Well, Miss, Margate's my fancy but I don't say as I wouldn't fancy a trip to Boulogne. My married sister went last year. Everyone talking French and the porters in blue blouses, most interesting she said it was. But would you believe it, Miss, she couldn't really get a good cup of tea there!

ENID. Tea is an obsession with you, Mrs. Huggins. I'd like to go East.

(She turns the pages thoughtfully.)

Wouldn't it be exciting Mrs. Huggins, if your life depended upon being able to invent a good story.

MRS. HUGGINS. How do you mean, Miss?

ENID. Like Scheherazade here. She was about to have her head cut off but she invented such a marvellous tale, that she was reprieved from day to day because the Caliph wanted to hear the end of it. What an odd thing it would be if one's life depended upon one's power of invention. I'm sure I couldn't think of a thing.

MRS. HUGGINS. I expect you could, Miss. It's wonderful what you can do if life or death depends upon it. Why, my sister Mary that weighs fourteen stone, why she went over a high gate as easy as a bird because there was a bull chasing her. How she did it, she said afterwards, she never knew.

(The doorbell is heard.)

Ah, there's the bell.

ENID. That'll be Mr. Strange I expect.

MRS. HUGGINS. Do you want me to stay, Miss?

ENID. No, I'll show him over myself.

MRS. HUGGINS. Very good, Miss.

(She exits to the hall. Voices are heard outside then **MRS. HUGGINS** *opens the door and shows in* **GERALD STRANGE.** **GERALD** *is an attractive man of about thirty-eight. He looks like a man who has lived an outdoor life. He has rather a diffident, boyish manner, which endears him to women. There is nothing bold or flashy about him. He holds an estate agent's card in his hand.* **MRS. HUGGINS** *exits to the hall.)*

GERALD. I – er – came to see over the flat.

ENID. Oh, yes. Well, this is the sitting room.

GERALD. Oh – er – yes.

(He displays the awkwardness of a man house hunting. **ENID** *takes possession of him in a maternal fashion.)*

Awfully nice. Quite cosy.

ENID. Through here is the dining room.

(She opens the door. He looks in.)

GERALD. Oh, yes.

ENID. Then through here are the bedrooms.

(They exit briefly to the bedrooms then re-enter.)

There – now you've seen everything.

(She indicates a chair.)

How long did you want it for?

GERALD. Oh, any time.

ENID. That seems rather vague.

GERALD. How long did you want to let it for?

ENID. Six months.

GERALD. Oh, that would do.

ENID. Do you want plate and linen?

GERALD. Plate and linen?

ENID. Yes.

GERALD. Well, I suppose I need plates to eat off – but I could buy them.

ENID. *(Smiling.)* No, no, I mean silver. Knives, forks, and spoons?

GERALD. Oh, yes please.

ENID. And linen? Sheets and pillow cases?

GERALD. Oh, rather.

    (A pause.)

    (Disarmingly.) I say, I must seem a complete ass, but you see I've never taken a flat before.

ENID. Oh?

GERALD. No. I left this country when I was nineteen. I went to South Africa first and then to Canada. For the last ten years I've lived in a wooden shack miles from anywhere. So, you see, you've got to forgive me if I'm not very – well – civilised.

ENID. It's rather nice not to be civilised. There's too much civilisation.

GERALD. Most women don't think so.

ENID. Don't they?

GERALD. No, women like living soft. They like cushions and things. They hate adventure or roughing it.

ENID. I don't think that's true. Most women don't get the chance of adventures.

GERALD. If they had the chance they'd turn it down.

ENID. No, they wouldn't.

GERALD. Well, more of them would.

    (He looks around.)

You know this is a jolly little place. It's got a nice homely feeling to it. Do you live here all alone?

ENID. No. I share it with a friend. She's out just now.

GERALD. Have you had it long?

ENID. Five years.

GERALD. It's just the sort of place I've thought about having out there. You said I was vague just now, but you see I haven't any real plans. I just thought I'd take a little place in London and have a good time – and look round and decide what I really wanted to do.

ENID. I see.

GERALD. (*Confidentially.*) You've no idea how exciting it is to be in London after all these years. All the time I've been out there, working like a dog, I've been promising myself a wonderful time one day when I made good. Sometimes I didn't believe it would ever happen. But it has. I struck it lucky and here I am – in London with money to burn!

ENID. It must be rather thrilling.

GERALD. You know how it is when one looks forward to things – plans the things one is going to do.

ENID. Oh, yes, I know! I've done it for years! All the time I've been grinding away in an office, I was always planning what I'd do if I had some money of my own – though I never thought I should have. And then, quite suddenly, like a fairy tale, it happened. An old cousin, whom I had hardly ever heard of, died and left me quite a lot of money – five thousand pounds of my very own. It was like a fairy tale, wasn't it?

GERALD. I know – the sort of thing one feels doesn't happen.

(*A pause.*)

If it isn't awful impertinence to ask: what are you going to do with it? I mean, are you going to travel, or what?

(**ENID**'s *manner changes.*)

ENID. I'm going to get married.

GERALD. Oh, I see. You're engaged.

ENID. Yes.

GERALD. (*Constrained.*) I hope you'll be most awfully happy.

ENID. Thank you.

(There is an embarrassed pause.)

GERALD. Have you known him long?

ENID. Nine years.

GERALD. Oh, I see.

(Another pause.)

ENID. We've been engaged a long time – seven years. He's been away in Malay. As a matter of fact, he's arriving back today.

GERALD. Oh, look here, I'm keeping you. I ought to clear out.

ENID. Oh, no. He can't possibly be here before half past twelve.

*(**GERALD** watches her very intently.)*

GERALD. You must be awfully excited about seeing him again.

ENID. Oh, yes, of course.

*(She becomes uneasy under **GERALD**'s continued gaze.)*

Please – don't look at me like that.

GERALD. I'm sorry.

(A pause.)

But, you know, you're not very happy.

ENID. *(Sharply.)* What do you –

GERALD. I know, I've no right to say that. But it is true. You're not excited about this fellow coming back. You're not in love with him. Any fool can see that.

ENID. Really, Mr. Strange!

GERALD. Oh, be angry! Be as angry as you damn well please. It won't hurt me. In a minute or two I'm going out of your life forever. You'll never see or hear of me again, except for reading my name on the agreement, or on the cheque for the rent. However angry you are, it won't hurt me.

(A pause.)

Are you angry?

ENID. Of course.

GERALD. I see. But it isn't only cheek on my part. You see, I thought you mightn't know yourself. Girls don't always and – and – oh, I'm being a damned fool but – well – the real thing will come along – and then...

ENID. How do you know that this isn't the real thing?

GERALD. *(Gravely.)* Just because it isn't.

(He looks at her intensely.)

You know it isn't. Don't you?

ENID. Oh, I –

GERALD. You see. I have been through the same sort of thing myself. I mean there have been girls – often nice girls – we have hit it off together and everything seemed frightfully suitable and all that. And I've thought – well, why not? Settle down and be happy. Nice girl, a lot in common, like her awfully etc., etc. All so easy. And yet, all along I've known that one day – one day when I least expected it, I would walk into a room and see a girl and it would be all over like that –

(He snaps his fingers.)

– in a minute. I would know – it was she for me and no other.

ENID. You think that will really happen?

GERALD. *(Significantly.)* It has happened – today...

(A pause.)

ENID. You must be mad!

GERALD. No, not mad. It usually happens that way. Ask the next half dozen men you meet. They will nearly all tell you that they made up their minds the first second but, of course, they didn't blurt it out like me. No, they played tennis with the girl and danced with the girl and talked about books with her. And then they found they liked oysters and hated caviar, and that made a bond.

Oh, all the usual gambit. I daresay I would have done the same if – if it had been any good. Only you told me, almost at once, that you were engaged and – well – that knocked things out. Didn't you notice that – well – that it was a bit of a shock to me?

ENID. How could I even dream of such a thing?

GERALD. No, I suppose you couldn't. Then I said, 'I hoped that you would be very happy,' and you said, 'Thank you' – and by the way you said it, I knew.

ENID. Knew what?

GERALD. Knew that you weren't too happy about it all. *(Gently.)* That is true, isn't it?

(**ENID** *turns away. There is a pause.*)

ENID. Yes. It's true.

GERALD. You don't actually dislike me, do you?

ENID. No.

GERALD. Well, that's something anyway.

ENID. You don't understand. I've been engaged to Dick Lane for seven years – seven years – and he's coming home and we're going to be married immediately.

GERALD. I see. Of course, if you really feel like that about it.

ENID. What else can I feel about it?

GERALD. Well, of course, the simplest thing from my point of view, would be for me to get a special licence and then you could marry me tomorrow. But, of course, you wouldn't want to do that. It wouldn't be fair on a girl. I can see that. I mean, you've got to get to know me a bit and observe my faults. I have got a brute of a temper you know. And make sure that I don't eat with my knife or blow my nose in a way you don't like. One can't be too careful about small things. And then, if it was all right and you felt you could bear me – why then...

ENID. Yes?

GERALD. Why then, we wouldn't take a flat, we would have a cottage – a cottage in the country with lots of those pink and blue things, what do you call them, lupins in the garden. And there would be honeysuckle and jasmine and roses and we would sit outside in the evenings and listen to the nightingales – just you and me.

(*He laughs suddenly.*)

Mosquitoes would bite us and the roof would leak – and there would be no drains and no hot water – but we wouldn't care.

(**ENID** *speaks low, almost fascinated.*)

ENID. You're mad.

GERALD. Well, why not? What is the use of living at all if you aren't mad – or what the world calls mad.

ENID. This is all great nonsense. (*Firmly.*) Great nonsense.

GERALD. I see.

ENID. (*Sharply.*) What do you see?

GERALD. You're going through with it.

ENID. There's nothing else to be done.

GERALD. Isn't there?

ENID. Why, half an hour ago I had never met you.

GERALD. (*Softly.*) I know, that's what's so wonderful.

ENID. (*Desperately.*) These things – these things don't happen.

GERALD. Oh, they do, my dear. You have happened – to me. You know that.

(*He takes her hand.*)

You do know it – don't you?

ENID. (*Protesting.*) Please.

GERALD. I only want you to say you know it.

(*A pause.*)

ENID. I know it.

GERALD. (*Gently.*) That's all then.

(*He releases her.*)

Well, I'm going.

(He takes a card from his pocket and writes on it.)

But look here, I'm going to leave you a telephone number in case – just in case you change your mind. Ring up and leave a message to say you'll come and lunch with me at the Savoy. That will mean that you're willing to get to know me better.

(He gives her the card. She takes it without speaking. GERALD *makes to exit but stops and turns.)*

(Shyly.) I say, what's your name?

ENID. Enid.

GERALD. Enid. Mine is Gerald.

(He exits to the hall. The front door is heard. ENID *stands quite still for some moments, uncertain, bewildered. The key is heard in the front door.* DORIS *enters from the hall with several parcels.)*

DORIS. Well, have you let the flat? I passed a very good looking man on the stairs going down. Was that Mr. Strange?

ENID. Yes, it must have been. He's just gone.

DORIS. Has he taken the flat?

ENID. I – I don't know.

DORIS. You don't know?

ENID. Yes – I – I think he has.

DORIS. For how long?

ENID. He didn't say.

DORIS. But didn't you ask him?

ENID. Yes. I – I think I did.

DORIS. Enid, what's the matter with you? You look positively batty.

ENID. I'm sorry.

DORIS. Does he want plate and linen?

ENID. Yes – he does.

DORIS. Well, you must be in love all right! You couldn't be such a complete idiot if you weren't.

> *(The doorbell is heard.)*

Hello, there's the bell. If that's your young man, I'll let him in.

> *(She exits to the hall. The front door is heard.)*

(Offstage.) Yes, she's in there waiting for you.

> **(DICK LANE** *enters from the hall. He is a gentle man of thirty-five, looking older than his years. He stoops a little and has a diffident manner.)*

DICK. *(Embarrassed.)* Why – Enid!

ENID. Dick!

> *(They shake hands, give an awkward laugh then exchange a rather uncertain kiss.* **DICK** *shows some relief that the meeting is over.)*

DICK. Ah!

ENID. Sit down.

> *(They sit nervously and take each other in.)*

I hope you had a good journey.

DICK. Yes, the weather was delightfully calm. We had it rather rough in the Bay though.

ENID. The Bay of Biscay?

DICK. Yes, the Bay of Biscay.

ENID. Did you have nice people on board?

DICK. A very nice lot indeed. I won the prize for Bull Board.

ENID. Oh, I'm so glad.

> *(Pause.)*

DICK. *(Awkwardly.)* Well, my dear, you look just the same. You've hardly changed at all.

ENID. No more have you.

DICK. A little greyer I'm afraid.

ENID. Just a little, perhaps, but it suits you.

DICK. Doris tells me that you have practically let the flat and that we shall be able to get married at once.

ENID. *(Faintly.)* Yes.

DICK. I was glad to hear that you had left the office. Of course, in any case, you would have done so after our marriage. I would very much dislike the idea of my wife working for her own living. But your legacy has made it possible for you to do so in any case. We must decide were we want to live now that I have this appointment in London. Wimbledon, I believe is a very healthy suburb, if not too expensive.

ENID. Dick – do you think –

> *(She stops.)*

DICK. Yes, dear?

ENID. Do you think we are going to be happy?

DICK. *(Smiling.)* I shall be very surprised if we aren't. Marriage is a risk, they say, but in our case, I think the risk has been reduced to a minimum. We know each other thoroughly, our affection has been tried and proved. We have the same tastes. I do not think you could find a more suitable couple.

ENID. Yes, we're great friends and we're fond of each other. But we're not terribly – in love.

DICK. If you mean –

> *(He pauses.)*

– mere physical attraction is not a sound basis for marriage.

ENID. It's nature's basis.

DICK. My dearest, real affection, such as we feel for each other, is a far better thing than – than –

ENID. Than the sex stuff?

DICK. Yes, if you like to put it that way. The affection we feel for each other has been tried and proved. It has stood the test of time and absence.

ENID. Words.

DICK. I beg your pardon.

ENID. Words. Just words – and none of them mean anything at all to me.

DICK. I don't understand you. Enid, my dear, you do not doubt my love for you?

ENID. No. I believe you do love me – in your cautious way. But I – well – I don't love you, Dick.

DICK. Enid.

ENID. And I – and I can't marry you.

DICK. Enid, my darling.

ENID. I can't marry you, Dick.

DICK. But Enid –

ENID. I'm sorry. I'm terribly sorry but I can't do it.

DICK. Enid!

ENID. I'm sorry.

DICK. Why is this?

> *(She only shakes her head.)*

Enid, tell me, is there someone else?

> *(A pause.)*

ENID. *(Quietly.)* Yes.

DICK. I see. I suppose I ought to have known that this was likely to happen. You are such a lovely creature, Enid, and I am a dull dog, I know.

ENID. *(Tearfully.)* Oh, don't.

DICK. I don't blame you, dear. This isn't your fault. I – I hope you'll be very happy. I hope this other fellow will be good to you.

ENID. Oh, Dick – you're so kind – so good. I feel dreadful.

DICK. There's nothing to feel dreadful about. This other chap – have you known him long?

ENID. No.

DICK. But you know all about him?

ENID. I know nothing about him.

DICK. What do you mean?

ENID. Just that.

DICK. But my dear girl, you must know something. Where did you meet him?

ENID. Here.

DICK. Here?

ENID. Yes. He came to look over the flat.

DICK. When was this?

ENID. This morning.

DICK. You only met him this morning?

ENID. Yes.

DICK. You must be mad.

ENID. Yes.

DICK. But – who is he?

ENID. His name is Strange. He comes from Canada.

DICK. I – I – I don't know what to say.

ENID. *(Gently.)* Better say nothing.

DICK. You're not the same as the girl I used to know.

ENID. Yes, I'm just the same. Only you never knew me.

DICK. Enid – you must do nothing rash.

> *(A pause.)*

ENID. It's no good, Dick.

> **(DICK**'s *temper slips.)*

DICK. The whole thing's absurd – absurd! I shall leave you to come to your senses.

> *(He exits to the hall. The front door is heard.*
> *A pause.* **ENID** *goes to the telephone and dials.)*

ENID. Mayfair 7593. Hello, will you take a message to Mr. Strange – Mr. Gerald Strange. Please will you tell him that Miss Enid Bradshaw will lunch with him at the Savoy at 1:30.

> *(She throws on a coat and exits to the hall.*
> *The front door is heard. A moment later, keys*

are heard and **MRS. HUGGINS** *enters with a parcel, singing*.)*

MRS. HUGGINS.

IT BRINGS YOU BUT TROUBLE AND DANGER,
TO LISTEN TO LOVE FROM A STRANGER,
MY VOWS I CAN NEVER RECALL,

(She undoes the parcel and pulls out some cushions.)

SO WHAT IS TO COME OF IT ALL,
BUT TROUBLE AND DANGER AND STRIFE

(She shakes her head then speaks to herself.)

Well, I'm sure everything's very nice and comfortable.

---

* A license to produce *The Stranger* does not include a performance license for any third-party or copyrighted music. Licensees should create an original composition or use music in the public domain. For further information, please see Music Use Note on page 3.

ACT II

(The living room of a cottage in the country. Three months later. French windows lead to the garden and another door leads to the kitchen. There is a fireplace with chairs and a bookcase. There is also a roll top desk, a grandfather clock, and a dining table with a tray of tea on it. **ENID** *is sat reading as* **MRS. BIRCH** *enters from the kitchen. She carries some letters on a salver. She is a thin, anaemic looking woman with a flat depressed voice. She has none of* **MRS. HUGGINS**' *cheerful pessimism.)*

MRS. BIRCH. The post, Ma'am.

ENID. Thank you.

*(**ENID** takes the salver. She looks through the letters and takes two addressed to her. She places one aside then stares, shocked, at the other.)*

MRS. BIRCH. Shall I clear the tea, Ma'am?

ENID. *(Abstractedly.)* What?

MRS. BIRCH. Shall I clear, Ma'am?

ENID. Oh, no, no, not yet. Mr. Strange will be in presently. I think you'd better make some fresh tea, Mrs. Birch.

MRS. BIRCH. Yes, Ma'am.

*(She takes the teapot and exits to the kitchen. **ENID** looks back at the letter.)*

ENID. From Dick.

(Putting it to one side, she takes her other letter and reads it rapidly. Then, slowly, she

opens the letter from **DICK.** *As she reads, her face softens with a smile.* **MRS. BIRCH** *enters from the kitchen with the teapot.)*

MRS. BIRCH. I've left the cold chicken ready and there's the apple tart – and there's a nice head of lettuce in a basin of water. Will there be anything more you'd like?

> **(ENID** *does not answer. She looks up and gives a guilty start.)*

ENID. I'm sorry, Mrs. Birch. I wasn't attending. What did you say?

MRS. BIRCH. There's the cold chicken, Ma'am, and the apple tart and a nice head of lettuce. I've put it all ready.

ENID. Thank you, Mrs. Birch.

MRS. BIRCH. No bad news, Ma'am, I hope?

ENID. Oh no. It's good news. At least –

> *(She pauses doubtfully.)*

Yes, I think it's good news.

> *(She looks at* **MRS. BIRCH** *thoughtfully.)*

Do you ever have dreams, Mrs. Birch?

MRS. BIRCH. Dreaming of snails is wonderful lucky, Ma'am. Dreaming of earwigs means calamity is coming.

ENID. I must try and dream of snails. *(Regretfully.)* I don't think I've ever dreamt of snails.

MRS. BIRCH. No, Ma'am?

ENID. Have you?

MRS. BIRCH. No, Ma'am. But there hasn't been much luck come my way, Ma'am. Watercress, now, signifies a false friend and to dream you are eating onions is a sure sign of death.

ENID. How do you know all these things, Mrs. Birch?

MRS. BIRCH. I've got a book of dreams what belonged to my Grandma, Ma'am.

ENID. Oh I see. *(Thoughtfully.)* Dreams are odd things. Doctors nowadays say they can tell a lot by dreams.

(A pause.)

Tell me, Mrs. Birch, did you ever dream about – about someone – and then get a letter from them?

MRS. BIRCH. That often happens, Ma'am.

ENID. Dreams are queer things. Everything's topsy turvy in them. You love the people you hate and you hate the people you love. It's – it's frightening.

MRS. BIRCH. *(Logically.)* They go by contraries, you see, Ma'am.

ENID. Yes, I suppose that's it.

*(She smiles. **MRS. BIRCH** makes to exit but pauses. **ENID** looks over the letter again.)*

MRS. BIRCH. I hope, Ma'am, you didn't mind my changing my day and coming today instead of Friday? You understand how it was, Ma'am, I hope.

ENID. Oh, yes. That's all right. One day is much the same as another to us here.

MRS. BIRCH. And I thought, maybe Ma'am, as you would prefer it, seeing as you are going to London tomorrow.

ENID. *(Surprised.)* Oh, but we're not going to London tomorrow.

MRS. BIRCH. No, Ma'am?

ENID. *(Curiously.)* What made you think we were going to London tomorrow?

MRS. BIRCH. Mr. Strange told me so, Ma'am.

ENID. Oh, you've got it wrong somehow. You must have mistaken something he said.

MRS. BIRCH. I suppose I must have, Ma'am. But I certainly understood him to say so.

*(**ENID** speaks more to herself than **MRS. BIRCH**.)*

ENID. I hate London. London is a stuffy place. Every year I've spent June in London, I never thought one day I should have June in the country.

MRS. BIRCH. We've had nice fine weather this year, Ma'am.

ENID. It's been glorious and this cottage is too adorable. Don't you think it's adorable, Mrs. Birch?

MRS. BIRCH. It's a nice little place, Ma'am – if you don't mind the loneliness. You would never get a maid to live in here.

ENID. Well, fortunately we don't want one to live in. But it is nice and so frightfully convenient with its bathroom and its electric light and everything.

MRS. BIRCH. Yes, Mr. Power, he spent a lot of money on it. He always said he would never get it back and that the place would last his time. And true enough it did and then sold for a mere song, as they say.

ENID. I shouldn't call it a mere song, Mrs. Birch. I think it was a terrible lot of money. Really more than it is worth, only we fell in love with it and felt we couldn't live without it. I think three thousand pounds is a lot of money for a little place like this.

MRS. BIRCH. A thousand pounds, Ma'am?

ENID. Three thousand pounds.

MRS. BIRCH. No, Ma'am. A thousand. It was in the local paper and I remember what it fetched.

ENID. (*Laughing.*) Well, I think we ought to know what we paid for it. Three thousand was the price.

> (**MRS. BIRCH** *looks unconvinced.*)

I believe you still think you are right and I'm wrong.

MRS. BIRCH. It's not for me to say, Ma'am. (*Remembering.*) Oh! I found this, Ma'am. It was on the path near the gate.

> (*She takes a little notebook from her pocket and hands it to* **ENID.**)

ENID. Oh yes, it's Mr. Strange's. He must have dropped it.

MRS. BIRCH. Yes, Ma'am.

> (*She exits to the kitchen.* **ENID** *looks through the book, smiling to herself.*)

ENID. (*Reading.*) Marry Enid, St. Peter's 2:30. Ridiculous boy!

*(She slips the book into her pocket as a whistle is heard outside. She swiftly picks up the letter and stuffs it down a chair. **GERALD** appears at the French windows. He is carrying golf clubs and looks very pleased with himself.)*

GERALD. Hello, adorable!

ENID. So there you are!

(He drops the clubs and kisses her.)

GERALD. It's a hundred years since I saw you!

ENID. *(Laughing.)* Not since nine o'clock this morning, in fact.

GERALD. Hello, is that the post?

(He picks up the remaining letters and flicks through them.)

Bill. And bill.

(Smiling, he throws them into the fire.)

And that's that!

ENID. Oh! Gerald, is that the way to treat a bill?

GERALD. Of course it is. We don't owe enough to be respectful to them. So long as you've got the money to pay them, you can treat them as carelessly as you choose. I don't feel in the mood for bills today. Tea very stewed?

ENID. No, it's freshly made.

GERALD. Good.

*(**ENID** pours the tea and gives him a cup.)*

ENID. Well, how did the game go?

GERALD. All right, except for those damned approach shots. I broke my mashie.

ENID. Oh, what an unfortunate accident.

GERALD. It wasn't an accident. I did it on purpose.

ENID. *(Laughing.)* Temper?

GERALD. *(Cheerfully.)* Temper. I felt better afterwards.

ENID. What a child you are!

GERALD. Am I, sweet? What have you been doing?

ENID. I picked the sweetpeas and I weeded the end border, and I picked some radishes, and oh – I don't know. It's been a very busy day.

GERALD. Did you get any letters?

ENID. One from Doris.

GERALD. Well, don't answer it.

ENID. But Gerald, Doris is very fond of me and I of her.

GERALD. She hates me like poison.

ENID. Well, you weren't very nice to her, were you?

GERALD. I didn't like her butting in here spoiling things for us. You didn't want her either did you? Come now, did you?

ENID. Well, of course – I mean –

GERALD. There, I knew you didn't. We're much too happy by ourselves to want anybody else.

ENID. (*Softly.*) We are happy.

GERALD. Of course we are. More tea, please.

> (**ENID** *pours him another cup. She hesitates, then braces herself.*)

ENID. Gerald, I've got a letter from Dick –

GERALD. Dick? Oh yes, Dick Lane, the fellow you were engaged to. Well?

ENID. He expects to be in this part of the world soon. He wants to come and see us.

GERALD. Why can't he keep away? We don't want him to start hanging round you.

ENID. He wants to be friends with us both.

GERALD. Well, I don't want to be friends with him.

ENID. Gerald, I believe you are jealous.

GERALD. Perhaps I am.

ENID. (*Smiling.*) Idiot!

GERALD. We're very happy together without anybody else butting in.

ENID. *(Seriously.)* Gerald, do you realise that I've quarrelled with all my friends on your account?

GERALD. That was inevitable. They didn't understand. They did their best to prevent us marrying. 'Why wouldn't we wait a reasonable time?' And when we took no notice of them, but just forged ahead and pleased ourselves, they got ratty about it.

ENID. I know but now – well – they are holding out the olive branch. Doris wrote me really an awfully nice letter. Won't you read it?

GERALD. No, I don't want to read it. I can guess what she says.

ENID. I can understand that you feel rather sore. Doris was very outspoken and really very rude to you. But all the same I think I'd like to answer the letter.

(A pause.)

GERALD. All right – but not today. Don't write till tomorrow.

ENID. Very well.

GERALD. That's a promise?

ENID. That's a promise.

(He kisses her.)

GERALD. You're a good girl.

ENID. Oh, Gerald, I'm so happy.

GERALD. Are you, sweetheart? That's good.

ENID. I never dreamt I could be so happy. There's not a cloud in the sky. It makes me feel quite nervous.

GERALD. Why nervous, you ridiculous child?

ENID. I don't know. In case something should happen.

GERALD. Don't you worry your pretty head about things happening.

ENID. I know. It's silly.

(She laughs.)

By the way, look what I've found.

(She holds up the little book given to her by **MRS. BIRCH.***)*

GERALD. Hello, where did I drop that?

ENID. On the path.

GERALD. How careless of me.

> *(He holds out his hand but* **ENID** *opens the book playfully.)*

ENID. *(Reading.)* March 26th. Marry Enid, St. Peter's, 2:30. Was it really necessary to make a note of that?

GERALD. *(Seriously.)* I always put down my engagements.

> (**ENID** *turns the pages.)*

ENID. May 11th. Move into cottage. You're absurd, Gerald.

> *(She turns more pages.)*

Anyway there's nothing for today. June 29th is blank. Why, no, you've got 9:30 written down here.

GERALD. Oh that!

> *(He pauses. A curious expression passes over his face.)*

Oh, that's only to remind me to develop some photographs in the cellar tonight.

ENID. At 9:30 precisely?

GERALD. At 9:30.

ENID. *(Curiously.)* You look as though something were amusing you.

GERALD. Something does, rather.

ENID. Tell me.

GERALD. No, you'll find out for yourself soon enough.

> *(He laughs. Then with a change of manner.)*

Now, is there any work to be done?

ENID. Yes. The lettuces want pricking out.

GERALD. Right you are.

> *(He exits through the French windows.* **ENID** *calls after him.)*

ENID. And the sweetpeas want staking!

GERALD. *(Offstage.)* All right, darling.

> *(**ENID** goes to the kitchen door and calls.)*

ENID. Mrs. Birch? You can clear away now, Mrs. Birch.

> *(**MRS. BIRCH** enters and begins clearing the tea.)*

Take the rest of that cake home with you. The children will like it. How are they, by the way?

MRS. BIRCH. Tommy has cut his finger to the bone – and Emma – she pulled the kettle over herself and scalded herself something cruel. And Mary, she's coughing something terrible.

ENID. Dear me, I am sorry.

MRS. BIRCH. What with my being out all day working, Ma'am, they don't get looked after, what you might call, proper – kind as the neighbours are.

ENID. I suppose your husband is out of work, Mrs. Birch?

MRS. BIRCH. No, he isn't out of work, Ma'am.

> *(A pause.)*

I've had trouble.

ENID. Trouble?

MRS. BIRCH. Yes, Ma'am. I'd as soon tell you myself in case you were to come to hear of it. A cleaner, straighter man than my Tom never lived – and comfortable and happy we were. And then out of the blue, as you might say, along comes a woman one day and 'Tom,' she says, 'And so I've found you at last,' she says. And would you believe it, Ma'am, she was his own lawful wedded wife that he had deserted.

ENID. Oh, how dreadful, Mrs. Birch.

MRS. BIRCH. Bigamy, Ma'am. That's what it was and they sent him to prison and I never dreaming of any such thing all these years. But you never know with a man.

ENID. No.

MRS. BIRCH. You never know, Ma'am, what's coming up out of his past.

(**ENID** *is struck by the phrase.*)

ENID. Out of his past.

MRS. BIRCH. Very happy we were. Not a cloud in the sky, as you might say, and then this comes like a bolt from the blue.

(*She shakes her head and exits to the kitchen with the tea tray.* **ENID** *looks after her.*)

ENID. Not a cloud in the sky.

(**GERALD** *enters by the French windows.*)

GERALD. I've done two rows of lettuces. What's the matter, sweetheart? You look very thoughtful.

ENID. I am rather. I've been hearing all Mrs. Birch's troubles.

GERALD. (*Sharply.*) Mrs. Birch? What is she doing here today? She doesn't come Thursdays.

(*He appears thoroughly roused by the matter.* **ENID** *does not notice his agitation.*)

ENID. Oh, there was some Beano or other on tomorrow that she wished to go to, so she came today instead. But it doesn't matter.

GERALD. (*Angrily.*) Doesn't matter –

ENID. What is the matter, darling?

(*He recovers himself.*)

GERALD. Oh, nothing.

ENID. You don't mind her coming today instead of tomorrow, do you?

GERALD. Of course not. Why should I?

(*A pause.*)

Did she say anything else?

ENID. She was telling me about her husband.

GERALD. Oh, is that all.

ENID. He had a wife who turned up.

GERALD. Oh, well, I don't suppose that's a very uncommon story.

ENID. But think how awful for her. She had no idea of it.

GERALD. Women never have.

ENID. Oh, don't!

GERALD. *(Surprised.)* What's the matter?

ENID. She thought she knew all about him. She thought she was safe. Does one ever know anything about anyone else? What do I know about you for instance?

GERALD. Don't be a goose, darling.

ENID. Why, but what do I know about you? There may have been lots of women in your life before you met me.

GERALD. Well, of course there were.

ENID. Gerald!

GERALD. Oh you needn't mind about them. I didn't care about them. I didn't care a farthing about any of them.

ENID. If I could believe that.

GERALD. What is the matter with you, darling? You're not being jealous, are you?

ENID. I suppose I am. Yes.

(She speaks as though making a discovery.)

I suppose I am jealous.

GERALD. How absurd!

ENID. I hate them. I hate them all.

GERALD. Nonsense.

ENID. But it isn't nonsense. Oh, Gerald, I know I'm being absurd but will you swear that you didn't really care for any of these women?

GERALD. Oh, yes, I'll swear.

(He raises a hand.)

For any of the women who came into my life, I have never cared a penny piece.

(He laughs.)

There, are you satisfied?

ENID. *(Smiling.)* Yes, I've been an idiot – a complete idiot.

(They kiss.)

Oh, by the way Gerald, what did you say to Mrs. Birch to give her the idea that we were going to London tomorrow?

GERALD. *(Shocked.)* London, what do you mean?

ENID. Well, Mrs. Birch said you told her that we were going to London.

(He convulses with anger.)

GERALD. Prattling old fool!

ENID. *(Surprised.)* Gerald!

GERALD. Sorry darling, but I do hate the tittle-tattle of old women. I don't know what I said. Perhaps something about it being better to be in the country than in London – glad we hadn't got to go to London today, or something like that, and she assumed we were going tomorrow. Anyway I think she's half-imbecile.

ENID. She's frightfully pig-headed. She would have it that this house only cost us a thousand pounds!

GERALD. Oh, she said that, did she?

(He darts a sharp, angry glance towards the kitchen.)

Well, that just shows, doesn't it? A thousand pounds. I wish we had got it for a thousand pounds. Well, I don't think three thousand was too much for us to pay – or rather for you to pay.

ENID. I think it was a very wise investment of my money.

GERALD. I would much rather it had been I who bought it, but unfortunately I couldn't get at my capital.

ENID. Anyway, I hope we have finished signing papers about it.

GERALD. The law does require a lot of formalities, doesn't it? By the way, I've got a couple of papers here for you to sign. Last bit of legal tomfoolery.

ENID. Oh, do you want me to do it now?

GERALD. Yes, better get it over.

(He spreads the papers on table.)

Here you are.

ENID. Where? Here?

(He hands her his fountain pen. She writes.)

Oh! It's gone dry. Bother.

GERALD. Dash it all, isn't there any ink?

ENID. You see what comes of you encouraging me not to write letters! However, you've got some, I suppose.

(She goes over to the writing desk.)

Oh, it's locked.

GERALD. There's a bottle of fountain pen ink somewhere – must be.

(He looks about.)

ENID. Why do you keep your desk locked, Gerald?

GERALD. *(Carelessly.)* To prevent you prying into my secrets, I suppose. Hello, here's the ink.

(He finds it on the mantelpiece.)

That's all right.

*(He fills the pen and brings it to **ENID**. She signs. He twists a piece of her hair round his fingers caressingly.)*

ENID. It's all so dull. 'Whereas' and 'Where-to-fore' and 'The first parties of the second part' etc., etc.

GERALD. And you call yourself a business woman.

ENID. I don't suppose I have ever had anything to do with law, business or house property. My work consisted in taking down interminable letters about tractors.

GERALD. It doesn't sound very thrilling. Well, darling, what's the next job? Lettuces being duly pricked.

ENID. The library books have got to be done up to go back to *The Times*.

(She collects several books lying about the room.)

One, two, three – there's a fourth somewhere.

GERALD. Here it is.

(*He hands it to her. She sets them aside and takes out another parcel of books.*)

ENID. Here's the new parcel.

(*She opens it and reads through the titles.*)

June in the Garden, Famous Murder Trials, The Life of Charles Peace, Modern Criminals. You are fond of crime and criminology, aren't you Gerald?

GERALD. Yes, it's a hobby of mine. I don't care for detective stories. Silly stuff. I like reading the real thing.

(*He opens one of the books.*)

A man like Armstrong – now, a clever man in his way – got rid of a lot of people unsuspected, I should say – had the criminal folly to keep a packet of arsenic actually in his coat pocket. I think there must be something mentally wrong with a poisoner.

ENID. Every criminal seems to have his peculiarity. Look at the American Bluebeard – McMahon. Apparently he kept souvenirs of all his victims and planned their murder beforehand, down to noting the exact time when he was going to do it.

GERALD. (*Chuckling.*) He was too clever for them, though. They hadn't enough evidence. They had to acquit him.

ENID. They got the evidence afterwards.

GERALD. Yes, but they hadn't got McMahon.

(*He laughs.*)

ENID. I wonder where he is and what he is doing.

GERALD. Still at the same game, I expect – fascinating some fool of a woman. God! How they fell for him.

ENID. He must have been a horrible brute.

GERALD. Not he. A fascinating fellow.

ENID. Ugh!

(*She shuts the book with a shiver.*)

Go and stake the sweetpeas. I'll do up these books.

GERALD. Right you are. Come and join me when you've done.

> (*He exits through the French windows.* **ENID** *looks about for some string when a knock is heard. A moment later,* **MRS. BIRCH** *enters from the kitchen.*)

MRS. BIRCH. A gentleman to see you, Ma'am.

> (*She stands aside and* **DICK LANE** *enters.*)

ENID. Dick!

> (*She comes forward to meet him with both hands outstretched. She is clearly delighted.* **DICK** *looks different somehow – more alive.*)

DICK. Enid!

ENID. My dear, how surprising. I've only just got your letter.

DICK. I know. After I posted it last night I – well – I found I had expressed myself badly. I thought I'd just run down and look you up.

ENID. I'm very glad to see you. You do look well, Dick.

DICK. And you. You look – well – words fail me.

ENID. Well, come and sit down.

> (*They sit. There is a rather awkward pause.*)

Your letter – Dick – I – I was so glad to get it.

DICK. (*Eagerly.*) Were you? It was a rotten letter, though. I – I couldn't put into it a quarter of what I wanted to say. I'm such an inarticulate sort of fellow, Enid.

ENID. No, you're not.

DICK. I am. I always have been. I'm so damnably shy, you know. It's a frightful curse to go through life with. You make an ass of yourself – and you know you are making an ass of yourself – but you can't help it. That's why after posting the letter I felt it was all wrong. I hadn't said what I meant to say, so I came.

ENID. That was sweet of you.

(A pause.)

You're very impulsive, Dick. You usen't to be.

DICK. I was always so afraid of making a fool of myself.

ENID. I thought – I always thought you were a very calm and deliberate sort of person.

DICK. That's what I wanted everyone to think.

ENID. I suppose – I never really knew you.

DICK. I didn't know you. I was – afraid of you.

ENID. Afraid of me?

DICK. Yes.

ENID. Why?

DICK. I suppose because I cared so much.

ENID. Oh, Dick.

DICK. You see, I suppose I must have felt deep down that you didn't care for me in the same way I cared for you. And so I pretended to myself that it was all a calm, sensible, sober affair – two people with tastes in common and so on and so on. I saved my pride that way.

ENID. I never guessed –

DICK. I was a fool. But don't let's talk of that. What's done is done.

(He looks around.)

So this is your cottage. It's very charming.

ENID. Isn't it?

DICK. You've actually bought it?

ENID. Yes.

DICK. You don't find it too far away – out of things?

ENID. Oh, no! The village is only a mile away and there's the garden and – oh, there's always heaps to do.

DICK. So you're happy, Enid?

ENID. Oh Dick, I'm ever so happy.

DICK. I'm glad. Doris will be glad too.

ENID. *(Worried.)* Doris.

DICK. Yes. You know Doris has really been very unhappy. I'm sure you haven't meant to be unkind.

ENID. It's Doris who is to blame. She was simply beastly to Gerald.

DICK. I daresay she wasn't very tactful.

ENID. Tactful!

DICK. But, you see, she is terribly fond of you – and – well – it was all rather a shock to her – the suddenness of it all.

ENID. Oh, I know. But she needn't have attacked Gerald as she did.

DICK. You must forgive her. She just didn't understand.

ENID. You understand.

DICK. That's different.

(A pause.)

But about Doris – she'll be awfully glad to hear that you were looking so well and happy and that everything is – well – all right. Can I take a message to her?

ENID. Give her my love. As a matter of fact I was going to write to her tomorrow.

DICK. Good. I was afraid you were going to break with all your friends. You mustn't do that.

ENID. If they abuse Gerald –

DICK. They all want to be friends with you both. So do I. That's why I came.

ENID. It was good of you, Dick.

DICK. That and to – see you.

(Their eyes meet.)

I must be off. I've got a date for dinner with a fellow at the Inn. It took me longer to find this place than I thought. Look here, Enid, can I come back after dinner and make your husband's acquaintance?

*(**ENID** looks a shade disturbed.)*

ENID. Oh, yes!

DICK. That's all right?

ENID. I – it's rather difficult to explain.

DICK. *(Reassuringly.)* Oh... I think I understand.

ENID. Do you?

DICK. I'm not really such a fool as I look.

ENID. You don't look a fool.

DICK. Thank you.

ENID. You know, Dick, you're different.

> *(She stares at him.)*

Yes, you're different.

DICK. *(Gravely.)* Perhaps I am. That's your doing.

ENID. Oh, Dick, I am sorry.

DICK. No, don't be sorry. That's one of the things I've wanted to say to you and funked. It's like this – you gave me a bad jolt – a bad jolt and I realise now that I needed it.

> *(She is about to interrupt him.)*

No, my dear, let me say what is in my mind. I've been thinking a great deal the last three months, Enid, and I've wanted to talk to you very badly – and even now I haven't got it all off my chest.

ENID. Yes, Dick.

DICK. Listen Enid, you were right to do what you did. Oh, I don't say it didn't hurt. It did. But just because of that it was good for me. I deserved all I got. Of all the miserable cold blooded fishes, I must have appeared the worst. You see, Enid, I looked as though I'd got into the habit of taking you for granted. And it's perfectly true that I didn't realise for one moment how much I cared for you, until you turned me down.

ENID. I was a beast.

DICK. No, you weren't. You were perfectly right. As I say, of all the cold blooded fishes – and a prig to boot!

ENID. No, no.

DICK. Yes, I was! But what I wanted you to know is that I really did love you – desperately – all the time. Only it was buried somewhere so deep in me that I couldn't get at it. I want you to understand that.

ENID. I think I do understand.

DICK. I lost you and I lost you by my own fault. I feel that if I had only been different, you would have been different. I like to think that if I had been more of a man, I could have made you love me. But we won't go into all that now. What I want, Enid, is to be your friend – and Gerald's friend too, if I may be.

ENID. Dick, that's wonderful of you.

DICK. *(Casually.)* Nonsense, quite natural! Well, what about it?

ENID. Well, the only thing is, Dick –

(She pauses.)

DICK. Yes?

ENID. I'll tell you the exact truth. It's what I've wanted more than anything, that you and I and Gerald should be friends. And a week or two ago I said to Gerald that I might perhaps write to you and suggest coming to see us –

DICK. And Gerald objected?

ENID. Yes, he did.

DICK. So he's jealous of me, is he? That's a cheering thought.

ENID. It's so absurd really. I mean, I know he would like you if he met you.

DICK. I don't expect him to dote upon me. But he's got the best of it so he can afford to be generous.

ENID. I know. That's why I was so delighted when I got your letter. But Gerald –

(She pauses. **DICK** *glances at his watch.)*

DICK. Look here, Enid, I must go. Suppose I drop in this evening at nine o'clock? Don't say anything about it beforehand and don't say anything about having seen me now. I'll square the old dame who let me in.

ENID. Do you know, I think that's rather a good plan. We'll rush Gerald. I've got a very nice dinner for him.

DICK. All right, Enid, you feed the brute and have him in a mellow mood by nine o'clock.

ENID. *(Laughing.)* I will. You are both such dears and I do want you to be friends.

> *(She takes his hand.)*

DICK. I'm *your* friend anyway – till death do us part. But you know that.

ENID. I –

DICK. Say you know it.

ENID. I know it.

> *(They are both somewhat entranced, drawn together by some emotion. DICK releases her hand.)*

DICK. My God, I could make you care for me still! *(Quickly.)* No, no, I'm sorry. I didn't mean that. It slipped out. Au revoir, my dear, till nine o'clock this evening.

> *(He exits to the kitchen. ENID stands lost in thought. She rouses herself and collects the parcel of books.)*

ENID. *(Calling.)* Mrs. Birch?

> *(MRS. BIRCH enters from the kitchen.)*

MRS. BIRCH. You called, Ma'am?

ENID. Yes. I – I shall want you to take this parcel to the post when you go. I must just find some string.

MRS. BIRCH. Yes, Ma'am.

> *(ENID makes for the kitchen but stops.)*

ENID. Oh, and Mrs. Birch –

MRS. BIRCH. Yes, Ma'am?

ENID. You needn't mention to Mr. Strange that a gentleman called.

MRS. BIRCH. I understand, Ma'am.

(MRS. BIRCH *gives* ENID *a comprehending look.* ENID *flushes then exits to the kitchen.* GERALD *appears at the French windows.*)

GERALD. Oh, Mrs. Birch?

MRS. BIRCH. Yes, sir.

GERALD. I say, is there any of that thing-a-ma-bob stuff – you know, bass?

MRS. BIRCH. Beer, sir?

GERALD. No, the stuff you tie up sweetpeas to stakes with.

MRS. BIRCH. I think I saw a roll of it here, sir.

(*She takes some out of a gardening basket near the fireplace.*)

GERALD. Oh, thanks, Mrs. Birch.

(*She makes for the kitchen.* GERALD *calls after her.*)

Oh, Mrs. Birch?

MRS. BIRCH. Yes, sir.

GERALD. (*Friendly.*) You have put your foot in it, Mrs. Birch. You've told my wife something she was not meant to know.

MRS. BIRCH. Me, sir?

GERALD. Yes, you know, about going away to London. Well, that was my little surprise, you see. She wasn't to know anything about it. Look here, I'll show you something.

(*He takes two tickets from his pocket and shows them to her.*)

Read what is on that, Mrs. Birch.

MRS. BIRCH. Imperial Airways.

GERALD. That's my little surprise. We're going to fly to Paris and buy a few frocks. Rather fun, don't you think?

MRS. BIRCH. Very nice indeed, sir.

GERALD. Mind – not a word! (*Boyishly.*) She's not to know a thing about it until tomorrow morning. Then I'll spring a surprise upon her.

MRS. BIRCH. You can depend on me, sir.

GERALD. That's all right, then.

> (*He exits back into the garden.* **ENID** *enters from the kitchen.*)

MRS. BIRCH. Is there anything more you'll be requiring this evening, Ma'am?

ENID. No, I don't think there's anything else.

MRS. BIRCH. Everything is ready for supper I think, Ma'am. I have put all the things on the tray.

ENID. Thank you, Mrs. Birch.

> (*She goes back to the parcel of books.*)

Oh, Mrs. Birch, have you got any string anywhere?

MRS. BIRCH. I'm afraid I haven't, Ma'am.

ENID. Bother. We never seem to have a piece of string. I wonder if Gerald has got any.

> (*She crosses to the desk.*)

Oh, of course it's locked.

MRS. BIRCH. Mr. Strange always keeps it locked up, Ma'am.

ENID. How tiresome of him. I wonder where the key is?

MRS. BIRCH. Oh –

ENID. Yes?

MRS. BIRCH. (*Meaningly.*) No doubt if Mr. Strange has locked the desk he wouldn't be likely to leave the key lying about.

ENID. I wonder why he locked it. We have nothing valuable.

MRS. BIRCH. Gentlemen usually have their reasons for locking things away, Ma'am.

ENID. Reasons?

MRS. BIRCH. My Tom, Ma'am, he had a little wooden box as he always kept locked. Not that I ever thought anything of it. And all the time, would you believe it, he has his marriage lines with his lawful wife and letters she had written to him and one thing and another. All the time, Ma'am.

ENID. Did he?

> *(She stares at the desk.)*

How queer men are!

MRS. BIRCH. You never know what they're thinking about, Ma'am. And you never know what's behind their lives so to speak.

ENID. Behind their lives.

MRS. BIRCH. There's nothing more, Ma'am?

> *(She is still looking at the desk.)*

ENID. No, there's nothing more. The parcel will do in the morning.

MRS. BIRCH. Goodnight, Ma'am.

ENID. Goodnight, Mrs. Birch.

> *(**MRS. BIRCH** exits to the kitchen. **ENID** draws slowly nearer the desk but then stops herself.)*

I will not be a jealous fool.

> *(She shakes her head and picks up a book from the table. She sits and reads for about twenty seconds, then lets the book drop on her lap and stares in front of her. Suddenly she rises. Going to the French windows, she peers out. She comes back furtively and pulls at a drawer of the desk. She runs into the kitchen then reappears a moment later with a bunch of keys. She listens and glances towards the window. Carefully, she tries key after key in the lock. Finally one fits. She opens the desk. Searching through some papers, she quickly opens a small drawer and pauses. She lifts out various articles, each one labelled. There is a handkerchief, a flower, and a piece of lace.)*

(Reading.) Mabel, Nov., 1926; Joan, April, 1927; Eva, June, 1925; Mamie, Oct., 1929. Mabel – Joan – Eva – Mamie. I hate them. I hate them all!

(She takes out a bundle of press cuttings.)

(Reading.) Trial of American Bluebeard. George Edward McMahon, alias Tom Lister, alias Gerald White.

(She thinks for a moment.)

George McMahon – George McMahon.

(She looks back at the labels.)

Joan – Eva - Mamie – Mabel.

(She looks puzzled as though she were trying to remember something. Suddenly she runs and collects a book from the parcel. Opening it she flicks through the pages and reads a passage out loud.)

(Reading.) McMahon was also suspected of having done away with Joan Edwards, Mabel King, Eva Garscheimer and Mamie Tring but no bodies could be found. McMahon entrapped his victims by going through a form of marriage. He then persuaded them to sign papers making over all their property to him.

(She stops.)

Joan – Mabel – Eva – Mamie.

(She stifles a cry.)

Oh! My God!

(She picks up the press cutting.)

A snapshot of McMahon leaving the court. Gerald!

(She speaks in a terrified whisper.)

Gerald!

*(A sudden noise outside makes her start. She replaces everything in the desk and locks it. She listens. Satisfied, she puts on a hat and hurries to the kitchen door. Just as she gets there, it opens and **GERALD** appears.)*

GERALD. Hello, where are you off to?

ENID. I – I have just got to go down to the village for something.

GERALD. Nonsense. I can't have you running off to the village. (*Humorously.*) I forbid it.

ENID. But I must go.

GERALD. (*Laughing.*) But you're not going. See?

> (*He turns a key in the lock of the door and puts it in his pocket.*)

And if you go through the window I shall catch you and bring you back.

> (*He laughs. A queer, rather unbalanced laugh.*)

Why, what's the matter, Enid? You look frightened. Has anything happened?

> (*She tries desperately to compose herself.*)

ENID. No, what should have happened? I'm all right.

> (*She smiles.*)

Don't I look all right?

GERALD. Yes, you do now.

> (*He looks at the grandfather clock.*)

Isn't it nearly time for supper?

ENID. Yes, it's nearly eight o'clock.

> (*A pause.*)

Just a little over an hour to nine o'clock.

GERALD. (*Sharply.*) Why nine o'clock?

ENID. I don't know – I just thought of nine o'clock.

GERALD. Come on, let's have supper. We'll set it together.

> (*He unlocks the kitchen door.* **ENID** *throws one quick glance at the French windows and whispers to herself.*)

ENID. Oh, my God! George McMahon.

GERALD. What's the matter?

ENID. Nothing. I feel a little faint.

GERALD. Nonsense. It's no good feeling faint.

(She tries to pull herself together.)

ENID. No, it's no use feeling faint.

(A pause.)

Let's get supper.

ACT III

(The curtains are drawn over the French windows but daylight shows through them. A lamp or two is lit. **ENID** *and* **GERALD** *are finishing a meal at the table. The grandfather clock shows the time to be twenty-five past eight.)*

GERALD. A very good dinner. That slab-faced woman, what's her name – Birch – cooks well. I was annoyed at her turning up today but I really believe, after all, it's all been for the best.

(He laughs in rather a curious manner.)

Yes, all for the best.

ENID. She is a very decent sort of woman.

GERALD. But not merry. Distinctly not merry. A sour-faced slut, in fact.

ENID. Well, she's had a lot of trouble.

GERALD. Trouble – trouble. All the trouble women get, they usually deserve. They've got no sense – absolutely no sense.

ENID. I expect that's true sometimes.

GERALD. Born fools, the little angels! Woman's weakness is man's opportunity. Did Shakespeare say that or did I think of it myself? I believe I thought of it. If so, it's good, it's damned good!

ENID. Have some more port?

GERALD. I believe you want to get me drunk, Enid.

ENID. What an idea!

GERALD. You've been pressing drinks on me all through supper. Well, I don't mind. Tonight's a celebration – a little celebration.

ENID. Is it?

GERALD. You mean, what of? I'll tell you. It's a celebration of three months of happily married life. Here's to it!

(He raises his glass.)

(Chuckling.) But you won't make me drunk. I've the hardest head in the States. I can drink bootlegger's stuff and never turn a hair. *(Thoughtfully.)* I'm a very remarkable man.

ENID. Yes, you are.

GERALD. So you realise it, do you? Yes, I'm a very remarkable man.

> **(ENID** *turns slowly to look at the clock. Her face changes. The mask slips. It shows terror.* **GERALD** *gives a sudden chuckle and instantly the mask is back again.)*

Yes, I'm a remarkable man. I'm – well – I'm different from other men.

ENID. Yes, I think you are.

GERALD. I've a lot of power over women for instance. I've always had it. I discovered quite young that I could twist women round my little finger. It's a useful gift. Boyish – that's the note they like. Makes them feel maternal. The eternal boy – it fetches them every time.

(A pause.)

(Suspiciously.) I don't know why I'm saying all this to you, I'm sure.

ENID. *(Placidly.)* Because you know I'm interested.

GERALD. Are you? Are you really? You know, one gets lonely sometimes. There's no one one can talk to about oneself. It wouldn't do. It wouldn't be safe. No, it wouldn't be safe.

> *(He broods then rouses himself with a chuckle.)*

But it's safe enough tonight. Oh yes, tonight's all right. I can say anything tonight.

(**ENID** *looks at the clock.*)

(*Sharply.*) What are you looking at the clock for?

ENID. I – was I?

GERALD. You've been looking at it all through dinner. Why? That's what I want to know. Why?

ENID. No reason. Go on with what you were saying – about your being different from other men.

GERALD. You wanted to run away before supper.

ENID. What nonsense!

GERALD. It wasn't nonsense. You did.

(*He looks at her suspiciously.*)

Why?

ENID. You're imagining things.

GERALD. No, I'm not. You wanted to get away. I felt it. I can always feel things. And you had your hat on and you spoke of going to the village for something. That's absurd, all the shops would have been shut.

ENID. I was having a joke. It was just fun.

GERALD. Was it? You don't want to get away now?

ENID. No. (*Bitterly.*) It would be no good.

GERALD. What do you mean?

ENID. It's too late for – for the kind of joke I'd thought of.

GERALD. You wouldn't get far. (*Laughing.*) What I like about this place is the loneliness. There's not a single house of any kind within a mile of it. That's good. That's why I chose it.

ENID. You thought of that – at the beginning.

GERALD. Rather. (*Quickly.*) I mean, that's what you want for a honeymoon.

ENID. Yes.

GERALD. Far away from anyone. Somewhere where we can be quite alone and uninterrupted. This place is ideal. Nobody's likely to come here tonight, are they? (*Fiercely.*) What are you looking at the clock for?

ENID. I'm not.

GERALD. You were.

> *(He leans forward staring at her. She stares back.)*

There's something you're hiding from me, damn you. I know it. What is it? What is it?

ENID. I must clear the supper things away.

> *(She rises and starts to pile things on a tray.)*

GERALD. I'll come with you and help.

ENID. I can manage.

GERALD. No, I'll come with you.

ENID. Why not sit and smoke?

GERALD. No, my girl. You might give me the slip.

ENID. What an absurd idea!

GERALD. Truth is, I'm a bit mad tonight.

> *(He speaks boyishly again.)*

You must put up with me, Enid.

> *(They exit to the kitchen with the tray. **ENID** comes back to take additional things. Alone, she casts a glance towards the French windows. She moves slowly towards them. Suddenly, **GERALD** is heard and she darts back to table as he enters. They take out a second lot of things then come back with a coffee tray. **GERALD** sits and **ENID** makes the coffee. She starts to show the strain she is under.)*

Yes, as you say, I'm different from other people. I've got more courage and determination – less hypocrisy. And I've got brains. I can think and plan. My plans are cast iron. Nothing ever goes wrong with my plans.

ENID. That's rather a rash thing to say.

GERALD. Nonsense. Nothing ever has gone wrong with anything I planned.

ENID. Someday, perhaps, it will.

GERALD. Never! I plan too carefully.

ENID. There's the unforeseen.

GERALD. I foresee everything.

(**ENID** *looks up at the clock.*)

ENID. I wonder.

GERALD. *(Abruptly.)* What's the time?

ENID. *(Startled.)* The time? It's – it's a quarter to nine.

GERALD. Ah!

(*He picks up a book and looks at it.*)

They say most murderers are mad – that they've got a kink somewhere. That's nonsense. A murderer is often a man who's a bit saner than other people. Don't you agree?

ENID. Tonight, I feel I don't know what sanity is.

GERALD. Is the coffee ready?

ENID. It's got to boil up once more.

(**GERALD** *opens the book.*)

GERALD. Armstrong was clever, but not quite clever enough. Crippen was a fool and he knuckled under to women. That's the most foolish mistake of all. Rouse was another made a fool of by women.

(*A pause.*)

Now McMahon...

(*He gives a peculiar self-conscious laugh.*)

What do you think of McMahon, Enid?

ENID. I never thought of him very much before tonight.

GERALD. No? He's well worth studying. He's clever. He never makes a mistake. Women fall for him every time. They come away to the country with him. They sign papers for him.

(*He laughs scornfully.*)

Most times he marries them – women like marriage, it's respectable. It makes them trust a man.

ENID. So that they sign papers without reading them.

GERALD. Eh?

(He turns sharply but is reassured by her calm attitude.)

What a time you are with that coffee.

ENID. It will be ready in a minute.

(She stirs it with a spoon.)

GERALD. It's twice as long as usual tonight. *(Irritably.)* For heaven's sake say something, Enid. Tell me something amusing. You've been so quiet tonight.

ENID. What do you think about dreams, Gerald?

GERALD. Dreams? What about 'em?

ENID. I know a girl – a friend of mine. She was engaged to a man and threw him over for someone else. After she'd married the second man, she began to dream. In her dream she was in love with the first man and hated and feared the second man. It's queer that. What do you think it means?

GERALD. *(Vaguely.)* I don't know, I'm sure.

(He looks at his book.)

ENID. I think, deep down, there is something in us that knows. We deny it and thrust it down, and in shame it rises up and shows us the thing we won't admit to ourselves is true.

*(A pause. **GERALD** looks up from his book.)*

GERALD. That coffee?

ENID. It's ready.

(She pours it out and brings it in two cups.)

Here's your coffee, Gerald.

(He takes it then looks at the clock.)

GERALD. Ten minutes to nine.

ENID. Yes, ten minutes to nine.

GERALD. We have been an age this evening. It's your fault, Enid.

ENID. Is it?

GERALD. Yes, you've dawdled as though you were – waiting for something. That's odd, *(Laughs.)* waiting for something.

ENID. What are you laughing at?

GERALD. I don't think I shall tell you, my dear. Not just yet. You will see the joke later on.

> *(She turns away to hide her fear.* GERALD *rises noiselessly and comes behind her.)*

Later on, perhaps.

> *(*ENID *screams and drops her coffee, smashing the cup.)*

What is the matter?

ENID. Nothing. I didn't hear you. I'm nervous tonight. I've been nervous all day.

GERALD. Have you? Have you really? Now, that's odd.

> *(*ENID *looks to the clock again.)*

ENID. Why is it odd?

GERALD. You wouldn't understand. If you knew what was in my mind, why then, you would know why it was odd. You see, I've got a plan.

ENID. *(Lightly.)* You're being very mysterious.

GERALD. I'm enjoying myself.

> *(*ENID *collects the broken cup and makes for the kitchen.)*

Where are you going?

ENID. To get another coffee cup.

GERALD. I'll come with you.

> *(She stops. A pause.)*

ENID. After all, I don't think I want any coffee.

> *(She puts the broken cup on the table then removes a volume from the bookcase.)*

GERALD. What's that you've got hold of? Oh! The *Arabian Nights*. By Jove, I wish it was a proper, unexpurgated edition. There's some good stuff in that.

(His face looks avid.)

It's hard to get hold of nowadays, I believe. This –

(He taps the book contemptuously.)

– this is only kid's stuff. What do you want to read this for?

ENID. I don't know. I took it out without thinking.

GERALD. With four new books unread? You're batty, my girl. Half the time you look as though you don't know what you're doing.

ENID. I don't.

GERALD. Eh?

(He drinks his coffee.)

Damn good coffee.

*(**ENID** takes up some knitting from the table.)*

My God, it's amusing to see you there knitting.

ENID. I don't see anything amusing about it.

GERALD. No, you can't.

(He walks about the room in a state of nervous excitement. His hands twitch. His face black and cruel.)

Do you know, Enid, that there are times when I feel like God?

ENID. How do you mean?

GERALD. When one has the power of life and death over someone.

ENID. I think the Devil might feel like that.

GERALD. *(Abstractedly.)* Eh?

*(**GERALD** talks to himself rather than **ENID**.)*

The secret of success is laying one's plans well. The country cottage – one can't beat a country cottage – and this has got a cellar – a very good cellar. I always make a point of there being a cellar.

(*He looks across at* **ENID** *and changes his tone.*)

That's where I develop my photographs, you know.

ENID. I know, dear.

GERALD. I am going down to develop some tonight – in a very few minutes. You are coming with me.

(**ENID** *stops knitting.*)

ENID. You said 9:30 in your little book.

GERALD. Yes, but I can't wait. I can't wait to tell you.

(**ENID** *gives one sharp glance at the clock and tries to retain her composure.*)

ENID. *(Calmly.)* Half the pleasure of a thing is waiting for it. Putting it off as long as possible – one enjoys it more that way.

GERALD. Yes, yes, perhaps you're right.

ENID. Anticipation, you know.

GERALD. Perhaps, perhaps. Yes, although often over too soon. One doesn't get the full flavour of it.

ENID. Oh, God.

GERALD. What did you say?

ENID. I yawned that was all.

GERALD. No good being sleepy tonight, my girl. We've got work to do. Very soon now.

ENID. Let me read to you.

GERALD. No, I don't want to be read to – not tonight. I couldn't attend.

ENID. Let me read to you about McMahon.

GERALD. McMahon? Yes, that's rather an amusing idea. That's a very amusing idea. That's a very amusing idea. Read to me about George McMahon.

(*He flings himself into a chair.*)

ENID. *(Reading.)* George Edward McMahon, to give him the name by which he was tried, for his real name is still unknown –

GERALD. You bet it is.

ENID. – still unknown, has a multitude of aliases, and has been popularly nicknamed the American Bluebeard. He was acquitted on a murder charge owing to insufficient evidence, although he was suspected of having done away with no less than ten young women. Not one of their bodies, however, came to light. The evidence against him was mainly that of Grace Alderton, maid to one of the few victims who managed to escape. After his acquittal, McMahon disappeared and three months later overwhelming evidence against him came to light. The bodies of five of his victims were discovered buried under the cellars of various houses he had rented. McMahon however, successfully evaded recapture. It is a terrible thought that he is even now at large. McMahon is a young and attractive man, certainly not more than thirty-five. Strangely enough, he suffered from heart trouble and the doctors were of the opinion that a sudden shock might at any time be fatal to him. His methods seem to have been simple in the extreme. Possessed of an extraordinary fascination for women, he would make the acquaintance of a girl, persuade her to marry him after a few weeks – or even days acquaintance – and then induce her to sign papers making over any sum of money she might possess to him. It was his habit to rent a small place in an out of the way neighbourhood. After living there for a month or two, he would explain to the neighbours that his wife was tired of the country and that they proposed to return to the city. The fact that the Mrs. McMahon of the moment was never actually seen to leave the place, seems to have awakened no suspicion. Yet, in every case the cellar could have told a guilty secret.

GERALD. *(Appreciatively.)* Damn good. Who wrote that book?

ENID. Edward Lawson, the K.C.

GERALD. He's a clever fellow. He puts things well.

> (*He chuckles to himself.*)

I'll tell you something Enid.

ENID. Yes?

GERALD. Mrs. Birch thinks we are going to Paris tomorrow, you and I.

ENID. To Paris?

GERALD. Yes, good joke, isn't it?

> (*He laughs.*)

I even showed her the tickets. Everything's always all right for me. I was born lucky – not a doubt of it.

ENID. It's better to be born lucky than rich they say.

GERALD. All the same one needs a little money from time to time. Yes – from time to time.

> (*He looks at her then suddenly rises menacingly to his feet.*)

ENID. Don't you want to hear some more?

GERALD. (*Manic.*) No, no, I can't wait any longer. I tell you, I can't wait any longer.

ENID. But –

GERALD. But I tell you I can't wait any longer! Come on. Come on!

> (*He advances towards her, now obviously insane.* **ENID** *rises to faces him.*)

ENID. No.

GERALD. What do you mean 'no'? You're coming into the cellar with me to develop photographs. Yes, to develop photographs.

ENID. Yes – you are mad.

GERALD. Come on, come on. Everything's ready. I prepared it this afternoon.

> (*A pause.*)

I'll carry you down there if you don't come and I don't care if you scream! No one will hear you.

(*He advances again.*)

ENID. (*Rapidly.*) Wait – wait! I've got something to tell you.

GERALD. I don't want to hear any trumpery tales now.

ENID. This is important! It's about – murder.

GERALD. (*Arrested.*) Murder?

(*A long pause.*)

ENID. Yes, that holds you, doesn't it? Murder is the only kind of story that would hold you.

GERALD. What do you mean?

ENID. Never mind. I know what I am doing. It would be a queer thing, wouldn't it, if a murderer were to marry a murderess?

GERALD. That's a strange idea. What made you think of that?

ENID. This.

(*She holds up the book.*)

GERALD. The *Arabian Nights*? I don't remember a story like that in the *Arabian Nights*.

ENID. Don't you? I think this story will interest you. It will interest you as much as the story Scheherazade told the Caliph. As I said, it's about murder. Gerald, it's about a woman who killed people and was never found out.

(*She sits, motioning him to do the same. He does so. A pause.*)

GERALD. Well, what are you waiting for?

ENID. I'm trying to get the story clear in my mind. It's a very important story for me. It's my story, Gerald.

GERALD. Your story?

ENID. I've killed people, Gerald. Do you understand? I've killed people.

GERALD. You!

(He is intensely interested. For the moment she holds him completely. She closes her eyes.)

Well, what are you doing?

ENID. Praying, perhaps.

GERALD. Come on, tell me, tell me. What's all this?

ENID. I must go back some time. I must go back ten years. I was a girl of nineteen. I was working at a wholesale druggist and chemists. It was poorly paid work with long hours. I didn't like working. I wanted to have money to be free and independent and do as I chose. About that time I met a middle-aged man who was very much attracted by me. He asked me to marry him and I accepted. We were married quite quietly at a registry office. My husband was a kind man, but very sickly. He bored me – but I never let him see it. His favourite topic of conversation was his health. He was always taking remedies and discussing their effect. More than half of it was imagination, but I never told him so. On the contrary I encouraged him. I made him believe he was a good deal worse than he was. To the neighbours who lived near us, I spoke of my husband's delicate and precarious state of health and how he was liable to die suddenly at any moment.

GERALD. *(Interested.)* Yes, yes.

ENID. You must understand that my husband was very fond of me. He was particularly anxious that I should be well provided for after his death. Every time he spoke of his death I cried. He became more and more worried about my future. At last he decided to insure his life for as large a sum as he could afford.

GERALD. Yes?

ENID. Well, you see, I always made his coffee myself. One night, after drinking it – he died.

(She pauses significantly and looks at **GERALD.***)*

GERALD. How much was the insurance money?

ENID. Four thousand pounds.

GERALD. Not very much – but enough. Eva had three thousand five hundred pounds. But did nobody suspect?

ENID. Oh, no. I knew exactly what stuff to use. You forget I had worked in a druggist and chemists.

GERALD. Yes, of course! That was a great advantage.

ENID. And that I had prepared the way beforehand. All the neighbours were fond of me and spoke of how devoted I had been. The doctor was a nice, unsuspecting man. He was very sorry for me because I was so terribly heartbroken.

GERALD. Ha, ha! That's good, that's very good.

ENID. Unfortunately the money didn't last very long. I was extravagant. I travelled. Very soon I had gone through it all. I went back to work in an office again. Shortly after that I met another man – also an elderly man.

GERALD. Yes?

ENID. We were married. He too insured his life. *(Pause.)* This time I got five thousand pounds.

GERALD. You used the same stuff?

ENID. Yes. I had taken a good supply from the druggists and chemists. I put it in his coffee. He too liked me to make his coffee. He said I made very good coffee.

GERALD. So you do.

ENID. I'm glad you think so.

GERALD. So that was your legacy of five thousand pounds. And then you met me! Ha, but I didn't insure my life for you. No, it was the other way about. I made you fork out two thousand pounds too much for this house. I made you sign other papers – papers that you didn't even bother to read. I didn't have to go through the bother of producing your dead body. You've made over the money to me as a deed of gift. I've got the better of you, my girl. You may be clever but you're not as clever as I am. You say you've killed people – you haven't killed as many as I have. Do you know who I am? I'll tell you. I am McMahon. The man they call the American Bluebeard. I have killed fifteen women, do you hear? Fifteen, and you're the sixteenth.

(The clock strikes nine. **ENID** *gives a cry.)*

ENID. Ah!

GERALD. What is it?

ENID. Nine o'clock.

(The doorbell is heard, then knocking. **GERALD** *turns to* **ENID** *furiously.)*

GERALD. So you have tricked me, have you? You've tricked me. That's why you have been looking at the clock all evening. But you shan't boast you've tricked me and get away with it. I'm going to kill sixteen women before I hang. Sixteen, do you hear? Get up and go to the door my beauty. Scream for help! I'll tell you for all your tricks you're a dead woman. You and your coffee!

(His voice changes.)

Coffee...

(Knocking again. **GERALD** *does not heed it, he stares at* **ENID***.)*

(Hoarsely.) Coffee. My God, I see it now. You've put the stuff in my coffee. Like you did the others. You've poisoned me.

*(***ENID** *is silent, staring at him.)*

You're going to sit there and watch me die, as you watched the others die. I can't move. My God, I can't move.

*(***ENID** *advances on him.)*

ENID. You can't move – already you can't move. You are paralysed.

(He repeats the words, almost mechanically.)

GERALD. I can't move. I am paralysed.

ENID. You can't move. I've poisoned you. You can't move.

GERALD. *(Whispering.)* I can't move.

> *(He sinks to the floor.* **ENID** *runs for the kitchen door. As she reaches it* **DICK** *comes through curtains at the French windows.)*

DICK. I couldn't make anyone hear so I –

ENID. *(Screaming.)* Dick, Dick –

> *(She flings herself into his arms. Her words pour out frantically.)*

He's McMahon. McMahon. The American Bluebeard. He was going to kill me. Don't let him kill me. Don't let him kill me.

DICK. My darling, it's all right.

ENID. *(Hysterically.)* I thought of a story to hold him, to give me time till you came. I was like Scheherazade in the *Arabian Nights*. I told him terrible things.

DICK. It's all right.

ENID. Don't let him kill me –

> *(Her voice trails off.* **DICK** *approaches* **GERALD.***)*

He hasn't moved –

DICK. He's dead.

ENID. He thought I'd poisoned him.

GERALD. He died of fright.

ENID. Oh, God!

> *(***DICK** *takes her in his arms and guides her out.)*

Don't leave me – don't leave me. I want to be safe.

DICK. I'll never leave you again.

ENID. Don't leave me.

End of Play

THE AGATHA CHRISTIE COLLECTION

Agatha Christie is regarded as the most successful female playwright of all time. Her illustrious dramatic career spans forty-two years, countless acclaimed original plays, several renowned novels adapted for stage, and numerous collections of thrilling one-act plays. Testament to Christie's longevity, these plays continue to engage great artists and enthral audiences today.

Since the première of her first play in 1930 the world of theatre has changed immeasurably, and so has the way plays are published and performed. Embarking upon a two-year project, Agatha Christie Limited sought to re-open Christie's distinguished body of dramatic work, looking to both original manuscripts and the most recent publications to create a "remastered" edition of each play. Each new text would contain only the words of Agatha Christie (or adaptors she personally worked with) and all extraneous materials that might come between the interpreter and the playwright would be removed, ultimately bringing the flavor and content of the texts closer to what the author would have delivered to the rehearsal room. Each new edition would then be specifically tailored to the needs and requirements of the professional twenty-first century artist.

The result is The Collection.

Whether in a classic revival or new approach, The Collection has been purposely assembled for the contemporary theatre professional. The choice and combination of plays offers something for all tastes and kinds of performance with the skill, imagination and genius of Agatha Christie's work now waiting to be explored anew in theatre.

For more information on The Collection, please visit
agathachristielimited.com/licensing/stage/browse-by-play

Lightning Source UK Ltd.
Milton Keynes UK
UKHW022050080120
356600UK00010B/648/P